Date Due

JUN 25		
AUG 11		
APR 02 '92		
OCT 22 1994		

JUN 25 7313		
AUG 11 20861		
APR 02 '92		

PUBLISHERS OF "THE COLONIST," VICTORIA.

56. Lieutenant Governor's Residence
57. Beacon Hill Park.
58. Agricultural Hall.
59. Beacon Hill.
60. Finlayson Point Battery.
61. Ross Bay Cemetery.
62. Mount Baker.
63. Cadboro Bay.

To Jane Leslie Touchie
a woman of compassion, love and sincerity.

Vancouver Island: Portrait of a Past

Rodger Touchie

J.J. Douglas Ltd.
Vancouver, 1974.

FOREWORD

When I first came from eastern Canada, I was captivated with Vancouver Island and wanted to know more about its people and its past. I was dismayed to find almost no material in the bookstores to help keep my interest alive. This was a surprising lack, for the Island's settlers have included so many well-educated people fond of books and of writing.

Records certainly exist; the Archives are bulging with material, particularly excellent photographs. Extracts from these collections, often enlarged to mural size, are gradually appearing in museums around the province. But amongst the summer hordes that patiently wait hours for a ferry to take them to the Island, there must be many who, residents and tourists alike, would like to see more — and to see it on the bookshelves.

I began research for this book, reading and sifting through the many photographs in Victoria and Vancouver. A Helmcken or a Dunsmuir or a lifelong resident could relate highly coloured memories and traditions of Old Victoria — and hopefully many will — but I felt that I could bring an enthusiastic freshness to my selection of material, and I trust that I have succeeded.

This is primarily a book of photographs selected to epitomize the quality and variety of life that the Island has afforded. It does not pretend to be a definitive pictorial history, but rather a portrait capturing the features that I found most interesting. I have deliberately written a short, almost encapsulated text to put the photographs into context.

And so I offer this sampling of people and events from Vancouver Island's past, this mixture of history, anecdote and nostalgia. I hope that it will not only entertain the reader but also engage him in further reading and exploring. I hope, too, that gifted writers trained in history will be spurred into recording further the Island's past in the way it deserves.

ACKNOWLEDGEMENTS

I am grateful to the pioneer writers and photographers who made this book possible.

My particular appreciation goes to my wife Patricia; to Edna Sheedy; and to the girls at Elan Datamakers who rescued me continually from typing deadlines.

The staffs of the Provincial Archives in Victoria and the Northwest Library in Vancouver have been extremely helpful, and my publisher and his staff, patient.

SELECTED BIBLIOGRAPHY

Andrews, R. W. *Curtis' Western Indians*
(New Press, Toronto, 1962)

Jackman, S. W. *Portrait of the Premiers*
(Gray's, Sidney, 1971)

MacGregor, D. A. *They Gave Royal Assent*
(Mitchell Press, Vancouver, 1967)

Ormsby, Margaret A. *British Columbia: a History*
(Macmillan, Toronto, 1958)

Pattison, K. *Milestones on Vancouver Island*
(Milestone, Victoria, 1973)

Pethick, D. *Victoria: The Fort*
(Mitchell Press, Vancouver, 1968)

Pethick, D. *James Douglas: Servant of Two Empires*
(Mitchell Press, Vancouver, 1969)

Robin, Martin *The Rush for Spoils*
(McLelland & Stewart, Toronto, 1972)

Rogers, Fred *Shipwrecks of British Columbia*
(J. J. Douglas, Vancouver, 1973)

Scott, R. B. *"Breakers Ahead!"*
(Scott, R. Bruce, 1970)

Sproat, G. M. *Scenes and Studies of Savage Life*
(Smith, Elder & Co., London, 1868)

Turner, R. D. *Vancouver Island Railroads*
(Golden West, San Marino, 1973)

Walbran, Capt. J. W. *British Columbia Coast Names
1592-1906* (J. J. Douglas, Vancouver, 1971)

ISBN (cloth) 0-88894-023-8   (paper) 0-88894-068-8

J.J. Douglas Ltd.
132 Philip Avenue
North Vancouver, British Columbia

Design by Reinhard Derreth
Printed in Canada

"A Man of Nootka Sound," from Cook's journals.
Provincial Archives, Victoria.

Illustrated in the 1784 edition of Captain James Cook's journals was the poop deck view of a north west coast Indian village.
Vancouver City Archives.

From Captain James Cook's *Third Voyage:* "A Woman of
Nootka Sound."
Provincial Archives, Victoria.

The longhouse interior drawn for Cook's *Third Voyage*, published 1784.
Vancouver City Archives.

All the British guns in Nootka Sound salute the launching
of the *North West America* in 1778, only ten years after
Cook charted the area. Britons were still few here, and
wholly occupied with sealing or fur trading, but their
territorial claim was hotly defended the following year
when challenged by the Spanish.

Provincial Archives, Victoria.

A painting portraying the 1789 "Spanish Insult to the British Flag." A landing party led by Martinez is shown in the dastardly act of taking an officer of the *Argonaut* at sword point.
Provincial Archives, Victoria.

In 1858 Upper and Lower Canada were thriving British colonies advancing towards self-government; the United States was preparing to admit Oregon as the 33rd state of the Union; and British troops were crushing the first major revolt in India. Isolated in the Pacific Northwest, Vancouver Island was a small British colony trying to cope with a population boom which had brought its numbers to over 10,000. The Fraser River gold rush was on and Fort Victoria was surrounded by a tent camp of gold-hungry miners.

Artifacts discovered on Vancouver Island indicate that the first visitors were of Chinese or Polynesian stock. The first recorded observation of the Island by a European was that of the Greek sailor Juan de Fuca on a Spanish expedition from the south in the 16th century. In 1774 the Spanish captain Juan Perez bypassed the Island, and four years later Captain James Cook, with his ships the *Discovery* and the *Resolution*, took refuge at Friendly Cove in Nootka Sound.

After a short stay, Cook sailed for the Orient with a brew of spruce beer and a variety of pelts bartered by the Indians. The golden sea otter pelts could be readily traded in China, and after this fact was revealed with the publication of Cook's journals in England, eager traders sailed for Nootka. Five-foot pelts soon were being taken in exchange for crude chisels.

Adding to the interest in the area was the speculation of many early sea captains that the Strait of Juan de Fuca or one of the many uncharted channels to the north might prove to be the gateway to the long sought Northwest Passage.

John Meares's *Voyages to the Northwest Coast* vividly described the hardships that he encountered when he sailed from Calcutta in the 200-ton *Nootka* in March 1786. The book's publication slowed trans-Pacific trade for a while, but the British persisted. The year 1793 saw the arrival of Captain George Vancouver by sea and Alexander MacKenzie "from Canada by land." Vancouver came to develop further the charts of Captain Cook and to explore the waters beyond the Strait of Juan de Fuca. It was also his purpose to resolve the question of sovereignty. The Spanish had established a military camp at Nootka.

Spanish expeditions to Vancouver Island, led by Perez, Quadra and Martinez, had resulted in the "Spanish Insult" of 1789 when Martinez commandeered the British ship *Northwest America.* The trading ships *Argonaut* and *Princess Royal* were also taken. By the time Vancouver arrived, however, the conflict had been resolved in Europe by the Nootka Agreement; the Spanish abandoned the area and paid reparations to Britain.

At the turn of the 19th century, the Russian fur empire extended from Alaska south to Three Saints Bay in Cook's Inlet. The "Boston Men" from New England were also active in the area. But after a decade of vigorous hunting, the otters were becoming scarce and the fur trading industry was waning.

Early in the 1840s, James Douglas, Chief Factor of the Hudson's Bay Company, decided to move his headquarters from Fort Vancouver at the mouth of the Columbia River to Vancouver Island. He sent a party to explore the island, and two Company trading posts were established shortly: one at the northern end of the island, the other, the new Pacific headquarters, at Victoria. The Hudson's Bay Company proposed to Earl Grey, her Majesty's Principal Secretary of State for the Colonies, that they be authorized to colonize and govern all the lands west of the Rockies. They settled for Vancouver Island, agreeing to pay an annual rent to the Crown of seven shillings, and Fort Victoria became the base for a 14,000 square mile "company island."

Under the terms of the Royal Grant of January 13, 1849, "The Governor and Company of Adventurers of England trading into Hudson's Bay" were granted an exclusive interest on the Island, the only major stipulation being that they encourage settlement.

Some Hudson's Bay Company shareholders paid emigrants from Great Britain to settle and farm the lands near Fort Victoria in a token effort to show Parliament that the Company was carrying out the terms of the contract.

The result of the grant was that all settlers were employed and controlled by the Company; independent settlers, especially from the United States, were discouraged. If the Hudson's Bay Company seemed an instrument of British policy then, it appeared even more so in 1851, when the British Parliament approved the recommendation that the Company Factor become Crown Agent for the colony. White settlers on Vancouver Island by then numbered only about 1,000 persons.

But even the powerful company could not keep out men who heard the cry of "Gold!".

So in 1858 when gold was discovered in the Fraser River and miners poured in from all over the world, Governor Douglas took it upon himself to license them and to administer the law.

England viewed the influx to the mainland as justification for the founding of a new colony and, after 1858, Douglas acted as governor of both colonies. Following the initial flurry of the gold rush to the Cariboo, the economy faltered and the colonies amalgamated to forestall bankruptcy.

The Islanders were bitterly disappointed when, in 1866, New Westminster, near the mouth of the Fraser River, was chosen as the capital. However, after a year the Legislature was moved to Victoria.

In 1867 Britain was very receptive to the formation of a self-sustaining colony in North America to stem the expansionist policies of the Americans, and on July 1, the British Parliament passed the British North America Act, uniting the four eastern provinces of Ontario, Quebec, Nova Scotia and New Brunswick to form the nation of Canada. In the same year, the United States purchased Alaska from Russia, and the crown colony of British Columbia found itself between two American territories, isolated from her eastern kin by distance and the Rocky Mountains.

As the gold rush and its inflated economy subsided, the British Columbia politicians faced two alternatives — be annexed by the United States or join the fledgling confederation to the east. The arguments of logic and economics favoured an alliance with the rich neighbour to the south, for why would anyone want to join poor, distant, disorganized Canada which offered only the improbable dream of a transcontinental railroad?

Yet in 1871, British Columbia became a Canadian province. Why? The Ottawa commitments to build a railway and to provide desperately needed financial aid were crucial reasons, of course. But there were other forces, partly generated by men like the flamboyant Amor De Cosmos and his mainland counterpart, John Robson. They saw the potential of a vast nation stretching across the northern part of the continent, and in legislative oratory and in their influential newspapers, they championed confederation and fought for their vision.

When in 1871 British Columbia joined confederation and Victoria became the provincial capital, the differences of mainland and Island became secondary to those between the province and the very distant federal government.

Joseph Trutch was appointed lieutenant-governor of the province of British Columbia on August 14, 1871, and called an election which produced a 25-member government with Justice John Foster McCreight as premier. McCreight's successor was Amor De Cosmos who succeeded in limiting the role of lieutenant-governor and concentrating political power in the cabinet. When the promised railway did not materialize, De Cosmos resigned and went to Ottawa to fight for action.

It would be 15 years before the railway was complete. Vancouver became the western terminus, though Victoria politicians had lobbied persistently for a railway bridge to the Island.

The Island was compensated by the building of a railway from Victoria to Nanaimo and by the construction of drydocks at Esquimalt. And, of course, administrative power was retained in Victoria.

Party politics did not come to British Columbia until early in the 20th century. From 1871 to 1903, B.C. had 15 different premiers, their governments being defeated regularly because of a lack of dependable loyalty. Between 1900 and 1903 the problem became acute, with five men,

from Charles Semlin to Richard McBride, forming governments.

Sir Richard McBride, "The People's Dick," established political allegiance in British Columbia when, at the age of 32, he assumed control of the province's Conservatives.

His controversial purchase of two American submarines for his "British Columbia navy" in 1914 propelled the federal government into providing coastal defences. McBride outlived one policy; three years after his retirement, a referendum of male voters give overwhelming support to the female vote, which he had opposed. The already shaky Tory government fell in the next election.

In 1917, under the first Liberal government in British Columbia, the new political power of the ladies succeeded in establishing Prohibition. "The Great Experiment" had begun, but it did not last long. When Prohibition was repealed, "John Oliver's Drug Stores" became one of the province's best and most predictable sources of revenue, and British Columbia became a haven for rumrunners supplying liquor to "dry" America.

John Oliver was premier for ten years; in his last session, he piloted through the House an Act providing for employer-funded retirement pensions. There was no federal Old Age Pension at the time.

Simon Fraser Tolmie, a Conservative, was in power in the thirties when the Depression swept the continent. The party could not agree on economic policy, and in 1933 the electors turned to the solid figure of a Liberal, Thomas Patullo. It was in this election that the Co-operative Commonwealth Federation, a labour party, became a political force in British Columbia. Although Patullo's Liberals captured almost 75 per cent of the seats, they had only 42 per cent of the vote, with the CCF getting 32 per cent. A split in CCF leadership prevented its becoming the government in the wartime economy of the early forties.

The war in the Pacific brought new fears along the vulnerable west coast, and citizens of Japanese origin were bundled off to internment camps in central British Columbia. On June 20, 1942, word reached Victoria that a submarine had shelled the Estevan lighthouse, but that was as close as the active fighting got to the Island.

An administrator among adventurers, Sir James Douglas
represented first the Hudson's Bay Company and later the
parliament of Britain as well.

This Colonial Legislature passed a resolution to enter into confederation with the fledgling country, far to the east, called Canada.
Provincial Archives, Victoria.

As governor of both the Island and the mainland Sir James Douglas in 1860 commissioned five administrative buildings for Victoria — from left to right: Land Office, Legislative Council Court, Colonial Office, Supreme Court, Treasury. Citizens soon dubbed them 'The Bird Cages'.

THE

Re-Annexation of British Columbia

TO THE UNITED STATES

RIGHT, PROPER AND DESIRABLE.

———

AN ADDRESS

DELIVERED BY

HON. ELWOOD EVANS,

Before the Tacoma Library Association.

Olympia, W. T., January 18th, 1870.

A year before British Columbia joined Confederation, she
was still being eyed acquisitively from across her new
border with the United States.
Provincial Archives, Victoria.

The Volunteer Rifle Corps and band mark the opening of
the Legislature in 1870, the last year of colonial government
in British Columbia.
Provincial Archives, Victoria.

Few frontier politicians in Canadian history could generate
electricity like Amor de Cosmos. As a journalist he greatly
influenced the Islanders in favour of Confederation, and
as a politician he worked vigourously for responsible
government and to assure B.C. its promised railway.

19

This Quamichan Indian village was typical of the Salish
settlements on the southeastern coast of Vancouver Island.
Provincial Archives, Victoria.

Chief Tlah-go-glass was clan head of this house at Alert
Bay. Visitors were posed at the right by Vancouver
photographer S. J. Thompson in 1898.
Vancouver City Archives.

Nimkissh village at Alert Bay. The living connection
between a clan's totem and the tribesmen was reinforced
by such ceremonial devices as the raven's beak in the
foreground. The lower half of the beak swung downwards
to admit guests one by one of special occasions, clapping
shut behind each celebrant. In this way the totem
symbolically swallowed each outsider who wished to join
the clan for a spiritually significant event.
E. P. Curtis.

Alert Bay totem poles, photographed around 1898 by
S. J. Thompson.
Vancouver City Archives.

A Cowichan carved figure.
E. P. Curtis.

Unlike other regions of North America, where the white man decimated the Indians, Vancouver Island was never the scene of a war. The Indian population nevertheless decreased. Estimates have it that between 1835 and 1885 the three major native groups — Kwakiutl to the north, Nootka on the west coast and Coast Salish in the southeast — decreased by 60 per cent to about 9,000, the diseases and alcohol of the white man being major factors.

Some Indians could foresee their fate. One Seshaht chief greeted colonial magistrate G. M. Sproat near Alberni in 1860, "...more King George men will soon be here, and will take our land, our firewood, our fishing grounds; ...we shall be placed on a little spot, and shall have to do everything according to the fancies of the King George men."

The coastal Indians were very different from the "Hollywood redskin" stereotype. Teepees, pintos, buffalo hides or feathered bonnets were not seen in their villages. They lived in large cedar houses, travelled in dugout canoes, and fished the seas and rivers. The women harvested clams, not grains.

Their religion was a form of animism; they perceived and revered spirits in living things and objects. Portrayed in their totem poles and often represented symbolically in ceremonies and feasts were mythological deities. One of these, common to all coastal tribes, was the Thunderbird. In the Cowichan myth, a young boy who had been an unusual child disappeared one day to return five years later with a strange glow about his body and beams like modern laser beams radiating from his eyes. He wore a strange hat which could produce lightning and thunder. He demanded many wives and received them atop a great mountain. In spite of their fear, two brave warriors attacked this god, called Scalligan, and one managed to kill him. Then, amid thunder and lightning, the spirit of Scalligan took flight in the form of the Thunderbird and soared into the heavens.

Extrasensory powers are named — almost personified — in the Indian heritage: an example is Tamanowis, the ability to transmit or receive thought patterns. Magistrate W. H. Franklyn, in 1863, told how an Indian constable of the Cowichans called Leemur sat on the beach seeking vibrations to tell him where a murderer had fled. Tamanowis led him north to the land of the unfriendly Kwakiutl, where the criminal was waiting helplessly for his arrest. The powerful Tamanowis had captured him.

The social organization of the Island Indians was complex. Transmitted in a rich oral tradition, it resembled a caste system, with nobles, commoners and slaves, but it was based on the clan. The number of clans was fixed; each was identified with one of a small number of mythological beings, whom the clan members saw as a spiritual common denominator, or ancestor. Since there was only one clan member — the head male — who could claim the status of a noble, the number of nobles was also fixed. Their power was spiritual and personal, rather than the power of accumulated wealth, and in tribal context it was closely related to the prestige of the clan's totemic figure.

One method of enhancing status within the tribe was through a potlach or distribution of property. To establish superiority, redress an injury, or repay debt, individuals would either give away or destroy their possessions. With time, the term "potlach" became synonymous with great feasts or celebrations.

Island Indian homes were communal, often sheltering up to 60 people. The Salish longhouse ranged up to 600 feet in length and was divided into separate family units from 40 to 60 feet square with a larger "end suite" for the chief. The Nootka homes were similar with a flat, rather than gabled, roof. To the north, their large square residences were often partitioned into four units with a communal area in the centre.

Colourful totem poles remain the prime symbol of the coastal Indians, although there were few, if any, poles on the Island a hundred years ago. They originated farther north with the Haidas and the Tsimsyans. The Alert Bay Indians at the northern end of the Island adopted the totem, but there were never many in the south. Though all totems portray a story they are difficult in interpret.

A ready supply of hard, sharp, iron tools undoubtedly helped the totem boom prior to 1900. Chief Mungo Martin was one of the most famous carvers until his death in 1962 and many of his masterpieces stand in Thunderbird Park, Victoria, and near his Alert Bay home.

Totem poles were not the only form of Indian heraldry, as the carved frontal poles, interior house support poles, dancing masks and family crests attest. Longhouse walls, too, were decorated with carvings of the clan's ancestors.

The huge, straight and rot-resistant longhouse poles and totem poles came from the Island's impressive cedar forest. Cedar was also important to fishing and travel; cedar weirs were placed in river beds to trap salmon, and large dugout canoes were used to hunt seals, porpoises and whales.

Before the arrival of the white man the Nitinats of Clo-oose were respected by all coastal Indians for their ability to hunt the whale. The preparation for the late spring hunt took many months; as important as readying canoes and weapons was the self-readying of the hunters, who together observed purifying rites and ceremonial rituals portraying the capture of the whale. As individuals they disciplined their habits; most restricted their diets, and the harpooner and his wife practised temporary celibacy.

Four canoes, each with a crew of six and a great chief to handle the 15-foot harpoon, would break through the surf. To the harpoon line were affixed mammal bladders which helped to show the path that the diving whale had taken. The paddlers would furiously pursue the whale, hurling more harpoons into it. Then one hunter would dive into the water to tie a line through the whale's jaw so that the prize could be towed home to a great feast.

Fur traders encouraged these men to turn their efforts to the sea otter and later to the fur seal. Then commercial fishing and crabbing were in turn.encouraged.

There were 7,500 Nootka people in 1835 and only 3,500 in 1885. By 1939 there were 1,605, and a last-generation recovery brought the 1963 population to 2,899. Of those, only 211 called themselves Nitinat.

Indian village at Quatsino.
Provincial Archives, Victoria.

Cowichan warrior.
E. P. Curtis.

A Cowichan girl of noble birth, dressed in a goat-hair robe.
E. P. Curtis.

Wedding guests, headed by a costumed dancer.
E. P. Curtis.

On a western Island beach, a whale is flensed — stripped of skin and blubber.
E. P. Curtis.

From his cedar canoe a hunter aims his heavy mammal-killing arrow.
E. P. Curtis.

A Nitinat woman boils whale blubber for the feast after the kill.
E. P. Curtis.

A whaler in ceremonial dress.
E. P. Curtis.

Nootka ceremonial costume of hemlock boughs,
photographed around 1915.
E. P. Curtis.

A Cowichan woman gathering bulrushes in the shallows
of Quamichan Lake, near the site of present-day Duncan.
E. P. Curtis.

Not all seal hunting was done from canoes; a careful
hunter could approach the herd along the rugged shore.
E. P. Curtis.

Poised beside a huge carved house post, a masked dancer
mimes the legend of a mythic ancestor.
E. P. Curtis.

A Kwakiutl dancer, acting out the unpredictable fury of
the grizzly bear.
E. P. Curtis.

A masked performer representing a mythical bird man.
E. P. Curtis.

A Nootka man photographed in 1915.
E. P. Curtis.

A granddaughter of the generation of Nootkas encountered
by James Cook — depicted with less artistic licence than
were her forefathers.
UBC Special Collections.

At Alert Bay, the goods to be given away in a potlach are
spread before the eyes of villagers and guests.
Vancouver City Archives.

A grandson of Cook's Nootka Sound allies.
UBC Special Collections.

This bastion stood at the southwest corner of walled Fort
Victoria in the 1850s.
Provincial Archives, Victoria.

A timber palisade on one side of the Hudson's Bay
Company barracks; verandas and glass windows on the
other. An inside look at Fort Victoria's entrance.
Provincial Archives, Victoria.

"The place itself appears a perfect Eden." This had been Douglas's impression in 1842 as he surveyed the site where he would build Fort Victoria. Indian labourers, mainly women, helped clear the land and build the fort under the direction of Charles Ross. By November, 1843, Douglas was able to report to Governor George Simpson of the Hudson's Bay Company, "It is in the form of a quadrangle of 330 x 300 feet intended to contain 8 buildings of 60 feet each." The fort became the company's west coast headquarters.

When the gold rush to the Fraser River began in 1858, Douglas maintained British control of the mainland by regulating miners and controlling navigation. To assure its position as the major supply centre, Victoria was made a freeport.

The boom brought problems of both excess and scarcity: an abundance of lawyers, transients, mud and saloons, and a shortage of shelter, women, water and drainage. It was 1862 before a man could buy a hot bath in the tub at Moses Delaney's barber shop. That year His Worship Thomas Harris addressed the first city council meeting after recovering from the mayoral chair's having collapsed beneath his 300 pounds.

Boom turned suddenly into bust. Victoria faced such economic problems in the late 1860s that even the public schools had to be closed, for there was no public money to help pay the teachers' salary. After British Columbia joined Canada, Victoria had still to deal with a depression matched only by that of the 1930s, and the city's population dropped from 8,000 to 6,000.

The railway, the sealing industry and the rush to the Klondike revitalized the economy during the "Gay Nineties." It was then that the Parliament Buildings and Empress Hotel grew around the waterfront, and the "Queen City of the Pacific" was confident as it enjoyed the McBride era and weathered the Great War. Prohibition closed Victoria's 109 hotel bars and saloons in 1917, but the 1921 repeal catapulted the city into the "Rum-Running Twenties," when Canadian-made rye was smuggled into Washington state, and occasionally eastwards, to the Prairies.

By 1932 half of the area's labour force was unemployed; Victoria's isolation from the mainland was a blessing, as she avoided some of the unrest common to other Canadian cities. Economic recovery during and after the second world war resulted in a healthy metropolis as it continued to benefit from being the provincial capital, and to attract tourists to its English atmosphere.

The beauty of the land adjacent to downtown Victoria and to the seashore appealed to the earliest settlers, and in 1858 Governor Douglas reserved it for a public park. The mariners' beacon atop a small summit provided a fitting name. In the early days, the 154-acre park was popular not only for picnics but also for horse racing. A two-gun battery was installed to protect against possible Russian invasion from 1878 to 1892.

In the last decade of the 19th century, John Blair was commissioned to landscape the park. His two artificial lakes have retained their original charm, but a park zoo was abandoned after many years. The caging of animals was not popular with the gentle Victorians.

During the gold rush to the Cariboo, the hotels and saloons of Victoria were the havens of colourful characters, the likes of "Washboard Mary," "Old Black Jack," "Dancing Bill," and "Twelve-Foot Davis." Davis would relate the tale of his 12-foot claim between two big, previously staked paydirts. He claimed the unstaked land and extracted $1,000 worth of gold per foot. An elaborate diamond tie pin vouched for his story.

Aside from the barmen, few merchants did much business, and bankruptcy was common. By 1870 the 12-year-old *Colonist* was reduced to a single reporter.

In 1878 the first wing of Victoria's City Hall was built, depression or no. After another ten years the clock tower, rising 100 feet above the entrance, was completed. During that decade the Victoria Theatre opened, Bastion Square started to take shape, and a horse bus service started with ten-cent fares.

By 1890 the Victoria Electric Tramway had four cars and four miles of track. The Board of Trade building became Bastion Square's new skyscraper in 1893, and construction of the Parliament Buildings and the Empress Hotel followed. In 1910 a million-dollar fire destroyed most of Fort, Broad and Government Streets.

After the turn of the century the causeway fronting the harbour became a speedway where constables used stopwatches to clock automobiles. Anybody who raced the stretch in less than a minute was fined ten dollars. Road paving reached the 700 block of Yates by 1912 and streetcars ran to Esquimalt. In 1913 Premier McBride attended the Royal Victoria Theatre opening. By this time, Johnson Street played host to loggers, sailors and sealers in the hotels and tattoo parlours. These were signs of the dynamics of a 20th-century city.

Established in 1872, the 27.5-acre Ross Bay Cemetery is the resting place of many Island notables: James Douglas; Judge Matthew Begbie; Joseph Trutch; 10 premiers and 28 mayors; Emily Carr; Billy Barker of Barkerville fame; Nellie Cashman, the miners' angel; Kenneth MacKenzie of Craigflower Farm. Most quoted is the gravestone of town character John Dean: "It is a rotten world; its saving grace is the artlessness of the young and the wonders of the sky." The cemetery has been called the "history of the province written in stone and marble and granite."

Oriental immigrants gave Victoria a flavour it shared with Vancouver and San Francisco: that of industrious Chinese labourers, opium dens, tiny theatres, lottery runners dashing down alleys, crowded restaurants, benevolent societies and secretive Tongs.

Many came from California at the time of the gold rush, but the majority settled in Victoria after the 17,000 workers of the CPR disbanded in the eighties. There were few women among them. The Chinese took jobs that no one else wanted, becoming cooks, gardeners and garbage men. They were highly regarded as servants for their honesty and loyalty.

The fact that the Chinese and British cultures did not mix readily in British Columbia is shown in two important political issues at the turn of the century: whether Chinese labour on public works should be restricted, and whether Chinese children should be allowed into the public school system. On one hand, the Canadian Parliament specifically outlawed the British Columbia opium exchanges in 1908. But on the other, formal restrictions on labour and schooling were only slowly removed. The patience and solidarity of the Lees, Wongs, Lings and other families prevailed, and the Oriental community below Government Street is now rightfully acknowledged as one of the city's most important assets.

By 1909, horse racing was very popular with Victorians. Klondikers, sealers, loggers, and the sporting gentlemen of Victoria — some 5,000 in all — went by bicycle, tally-ho, B.C. Electric Railway and the newfangled automobile to the Willows circuit. Four hundred horses and fifty jockeys raced despite Bishop Perim of Christ Church Cathedral, who denounced the meet. It took World War I to end racing at the Willows.

The Volstead Act prohibited liquor in the United States between 1920 and 1930, and Victoria became a thriving rum-running centre.

There was nothing illegal about exporting liquor from Canada, but the United States government revenue cutters patrolled the State of Washington waters to curtail illegal imports. To some Victorians, rum-running was an adventure, not a crime. The vessels on Rum Row in the Inner Harbour included 40-knot speedboats, soggy fishboats and converted steamers. Large "mother" ships left the harbour ostensibly bound for Ensenada, Mexico, but few went south of Cape Flattery.

Some found fortune; others, trouble. There was irony in the fate of smuggler Captain R. Pamphlett, who crossed into American waters with the *Pescawha* to rescue a sinking schooner. A revenue cutter intercepted her, and the entire crew was sentenced to jail in Portland.

Few buildings raised by Island pioneers have survived the years. Some — the Victoria homes of John Tod and Dr. J. S. Helmcken; the Nanaimo Bastion, and the batteries of Fort Rodd Hill — have been preserved as historic monuments, but the majority have burned, rotted or been demolished.

Of course, the most common and yet treasured of pioneer buildings was the log cabin. It was the settlers who fitted logs and fixed cedar shakes to their roofs. When thousands of sourdoughs tented in Bastion Square and along the ravine near present-day Johnson Street, a log cabin was the envy of all.

The beauty of the Craigflower Farm site was noticed first by the Spaniard, Galiano, in 1792, and 60 years later by Chief Factor Douglas. In January, 1853, Kenneth MacKenzie, the estate manager, arrived from Scotland to find that the promised facilities for his family and 25 labourers were barely started. Craigflower was one of four Hudson's Bay Company farms required to feed the community and provide produce for trade with the Russian Fur Company in Alaska.

The skilled Scots hand-hewed the beams and timber for dwellings, forged their own nails and baked their bricks. The manor house still stands as a testimonial to their workmanship. By the end of 1854 the Craigflower colony consisted of 21 dwellings with a population of 76. Of those, Robert Melrose is best known because of his "Royal Immigrant's Almanack concerning five years servitude under the Hudson's Bay Company on Vancouver Island." His diary records both day-to-day events and the philosophical arguments of the evenings. Throughout the text are estimates of his state of inebriation: "the author half drunk," "three quarters drunk" or "whole drunk."

The 600-acre Oaklands, two miles from Craigflower, was built at the same time by Thomas Skinner, and its 34 settlers soon harvested a fine crop of potatoes and wheat. Viewfield, also 600 acres in size, had been built in 1851 under Donald Macauley; Colwood, started in 1853 by Captain Langford, had close to 200 acres cleared and abundant stock by 1854. Food was plentiful until the demands of the gold rush four years later.

Grateful for their new life, the settlers made churches the centre of community sharing. Typical was St. Stephen's in Saanich. William Thomson donated the land for the small white church, and its first service was held in 1862. It still stands, and a simple greeting on the door welcomes all:

If you are weary
    Come in and rest.
If you are sad
    Come in and pray.
If you are lonely
    Come in and make friends.

Hotels were often the most conspicuous buildings in frontier towns. Such was the case with the Willows Hotel in Campbell River on Valdez Strait. Built in 1906 to serve the growing logging and fishing industries, it became world famous among sport fishermen. Until it burned in 1963 it was the home of the renowned Tyee Club.

The Prairie Tavern in Saanichton was a roadhouse built in 1853. When the Victoria and Sidney Railway passed by the door in 1893, proprietor Henry Simpson built the two-storey structure which became a popular refuge for weary travellers.

The Wheatsheaf Inn in Cedar started as a log cabin with a stand-up bar and a livery stable. Mineral rights, though never exercised, were sold on its site in 1908 by Andrew Mahle for $33,000. He had paid $5,000 at auction for the inn and 160 acres earlier that year, before coal was found in the area. Business thrived at the "Chief" until prohibition in 1917, when it reverted to a coach stop. After the eight-year "Great Experiment," it was reopened. But fire struck within the year. Undeterred, Mr. Mahle, then 89, towed two houses to the smouldering site and was soon back in business.

Robert Dunsmuir constructed Craigdarroch Castle in 1889 for $650,000 — close to $5 million by today's standards. The 20-acre estate was parted by a winding double-lane driveway, and the estate interior was decorated with hardwoods, Italian glass, crystal and no less than 35 fireplaces.

Ironically, Dunsmuir died just before its completion, but his wife lived there for almost 20 years. After her death the estate was subdivided and lots sold individually. The castle went for a dollar to the winner of a draw amongst lot buyers.

James Dunsmuir had plans for the luxurious Hatley Park well under way at the time of his mother's death. In 1911 the 700-acre estate with elaborate landscaping and conservatory were finished, and the Dunsuir family of ten moved into the magnificent home. After Sir James died in 1937, Hatley Park was acquired by the Canadian government to establish Royal Roads Military College. The low price of $75,000 constituted a generous gift by the estate.

In the early 1940s, Prime Minister MacKenzie King discussed the possibility of Hatley Park as a war-time west coast residence for King George VI and Queen Elizabeth, but nothing came of the idea.

In the 1860s, Governor Douglas authorized the construction of five government buildings whose unusual shapes earned then the sobriquet of "The Birdcages." Governor Douglas ignored the criticisms of his Legislature and stilled complaints of financial mismanagement with the terse retort, "It wasn't public money." He had raised the necessary funds by selling valuable Government Street property. The buildings served their purpose until four were demolished to make way for the present Legislature. The fifth was preserved until destroyed by fire in 1957.

Even the construction of the Empress Hotel a decade later must have seemed anticlimactic after the five-year project which gave birth to the present Parliament Buildings.

Controversy surrounding the $1 million expenditure was subdued only by the magnificence of the building when it opened on February 10, 1898. The undertaking was deemed a "British Columbia Project;" aside from Italian marble and other imported interior finery, it was constructed from materials found in the province.

Few hotels in the world are as closely related to the character of a city as is Victoria's Empress Hotel. Situated at 721 Government Street on the Inner Harbour, the CPR hotel was completed in January 1908, having taken four years to construct. It was designed by F. M. Rattenbury, the most prominent of Victoria architects, and cost $1.6 million.

The Empress was the brainchild of George H. Barnard and Captain J. W. Troup. After approaching CPR with the idea, Barnard entered local political life to assure community support for the project, while Troup set out to establish a sleek fleet of "Princess Ferries" to transport Empress clientele from Vancouver and Seattle.

Modern conveniences have been subtly introduced over the years, but the hotel's majestic 19th century character is still very much in evidence.

The long shadows of early morning fall across Government
Street in frontier Victoria.
Provincial Archives, Victoria.

Sailing ships, church belfries and a new James Bay Bridge;
an early, and misty, view of Victoria harbour.
Vancouver Public Library.

The fire department performs hose drill, 1887 style, at the
corner of Johnson and Douglas streets in Victoria.
Provincial Archives, Victoria.

Victoria's bars were guaranteed prosperity for the same reason that solid community-serving enterprises were guaranteed insecurity: the transience of the log-felling, seal-hunting, or gold-mining customers who made the small capital city their last stop on the way north.
Provincial Archives, Victoria.

Five-cent ales are enjoyed in the bar-room of the St. Charles Hotel.
Provincial Archives, Victoria.

A turn-of-the-century saloon, the Prince of Wales, on Government Street.
Provincial Archives, Victoria.

Victoria's Government Street in 1896.
Provincial Archives, Victoria.

Klondikers started passing through Victoria in 1897, and
kept cash flowing through the tradesmen's tills faster than
silt through sluice gates.
Provincial Archives, Victoria.

The Empress Hotel goes up, 1905-6.
Provincial Archives, Victoria.

When these substantial parliament buildings were
completed in 1898, hope died for the mainlanders who had
been pressing for New Westminster to be renamed British
Columbia's capital city.
Provincial Archives, Victoria.

A panorama of Victoria harbour from the roof of the
brand new Parliament buildings, showing the then
undistinguished site of the Empress Hotel to the right of
the St. James Bridge.
Vancouver Public Library.

George Barnard's vision of a magnificent meeting place for turn-of-the-century tourists culminated in the Empress's skylighted ballroom.
Provincial Archives, Victoria.

Racing fever brings throngs to the Willows track in the 1902 racing season.
Provincial Archives, Victoria.

Washington State's Olympic Range asserts the American presence in this southward-looking view of the James Bay Causeway in the 1930s.

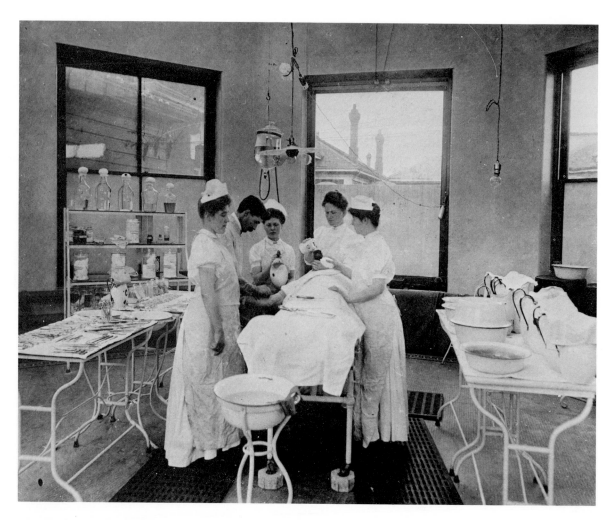

This Royal Jubilee Hospital operating room was wired for electricity in 1897. Daylight illuminates the surgery being undertaken here in 1906.
Provincial Archives, Victoria.

British influence remained strong for decades after
Confederation. The bobby-style helmets of the Police
Department helped to maintain the colonial atmosphere of
Victoria streets.
Provincial Archives, Victoria.

The performers in Professor Wicker's annual concert, 1905.
Provincial Archives, Victoria.

Yarn-swapping oldtimers, some of them veterans of the Cariboo gold rush, usually lounged casually at the Angel Hotel on Main Street, but 19th century photography called for a more formal-looking gathering.

Provincial Archives, Victoria.

Amor De Cosmos's editorial and political opposition to the
presence of Chinese in British Columbia is cartooned in
Canadian Illustrated News, 1879.
Provincial Archives, Victoria.

The youngest of these Japanese children thwart a Victoria
photographer's attempt to picture the whole group in the
keen-eyed repose of their grandfather.
Provincial Archives, Victoria.

Economic recession on the Island always intensified anti-
Oriental feeling. Even the much-loved Chinese New Year
celebrations were greeted in 1910 with this acerbic
commentary, copied in Victoria from the Vancouver
Province.
Provinical Archives, Victoria.

A quiet shop in Victoria's Chinatown, with even the
activity of the abacus in temporary suspension.
Vancouver Public Library.

Grade 7 and 8 girls receive sewing instruction in a classroom
of the Sir James Douglas School, 1912.
Provincial Archives, Victoria.

British Columbia's prewar premier, Richard McBride, was confident that the exclusively male electorate would always share his opposition to the female vote. His immediate successor found that this Tory plank would not hold him up through the 1917 election.
Provincial Archives, Victoria.

Gracious — and canny — in defeat, Opposition Leader W. J. Bowser hosts a garden party at his home two years after suffragette agitation helped to bring down his Tory government.
Provincial Archives, Victoria.

Victoria's spiritualists enjoy a picnic with their families at Cordova Bay, 1890.
Provincial Archives, Victoria.

Half of McBride's "British Columbia Navy" purchased
from the United States in 1914 to embarrass the federal
defence department into protecting the vulnerable Pacific
coast.
Provincial Archives, Victoria.

November 11, 1918. The Great War is over and Victoria
rejoices in anticipation of the boys' all coming home.
Provincial Archives, Victoria.

May 8, 1915: Onlookers give a benign front to Victoria's
riot of vengeance for the sinking of the *Lusitania*. The
crowd has wrecked the interior of the Kaiserhof Hotel
after demolishing a German club on Government Street.
Soldiers have just taken protective positions around the
hotel, although this is the crowd's second visit.
Provincial Archives, Victoria.

A platform stands ready for patriotic speeches at a Victoria
garden party, 1914.
Provincial Archives, Victoria.

Men in the uniforms of World War I mingle with voters
checking the results of a June, 1918, by-election.
Provincial Archives, Victoria.

Hatley Park was the magnificent estate of James Dunsmuir
after 1911 and the scene of Victoria's most prestigious
social events.

The shoeless Coal Tyee, honoured for leading a Hudson's
Bay Company man to the coal deposits of Nanaimo, poses
with his sternfaced retinue.
Provincial Archives, Victoria.

When the Hudson's Bay Company expanded its empire to Vancouver Island, it was not only for furs and trade with the Indians. In 1835, Dr. W. F. Tolmie had discovered coal on the northern end of Vancouver Island. This find was important despite Fort Rupert's low grade of the seam because demand for coal existed in California. The Indians of the area were very unfriendly and in 1849 a stockade was built to protect the miners. This venture died, however, when high-quality coal was discovered elsewhere.

A Nanaimo Indian, Che-wech-i-kan, in 1845 casually remarked to a Fort Victoria blacksmith that he knew of black rock like that which the blacksmith used to fire the forge. Led by Che-wech-i-kan, the Hudson's Bay Company clerk Joseph Mackay discovered the huge Nanaimo coal beds. The Indian was rewarded with a bottle of rum, the repair of his musket, and the title "Coal Tyee" or "Coal chief." Chief Factor Douglas authorized MacKay "to proceed with all possible diligence to...Nanymo and formally take possession of the coal beds lately discovered."

By 1858 miners had been brought around Cape Horn from England, and 125 inhabitants lived in the thriving little company town. Coal had become one of the Island's major sources of income. The Hudson's Bay Company concentrated on surface mining until its interests were bought out in 1862 for 40,000 pounds by the newly formed Vancouver Coal Mining and Land Company. More sophisticated methods of extracting the rich but sulphurous coal were developed, and large cargoes were exported to San Francisco.

A second major company sprang up in 1871 after the Scottish miner, Robert Dunsmuir, found rich deposits at Wellington. Soon he was rich enough to build the castle that he had promised his bride 20 years before when they arrived at Fort Rupert.

The Nanaimo coal fields were particularly dangerous because of the prevalence of gas pockets. On May 3, 1887, an explosion in "Old Number One," the main shaft, killed 150 men. Only seven members of the entire afternoon shift survived. Listed amongst the dead were "Chinamen, names unknown, numbers 3, 71, 72."

The Nanaimo Bastion flag flies at half mast every May 3 in remembrance of that day. Seven months after the Number One shaft disaster, 77 men perished in an explosion at the Dunsmuir Wellington mine. There were many more explosions, more than 300 miners being killed over the years. The last Island coal mine, Tsable River Mine near Comox, closed in 1966. Labour disputes, tragedies, faltering markets and the gradual depletion of the mineral all had taken their toll.

In 1863, in an effort to stimulate the faltering Island economy, Governor Arthur Kennedy promoted an expedition to seek out mineral wealth. The next year, an ex-Royal Engineer in the expedition, Peter Leech, found gold in what is now Leech River and lesser traces in the mainstream, the Sooke River.

The Colonist published the news and soon prospectors were streaming to the discovery site, only ten miles distant, from Victoria. Within six months there were 1,200 miners in the tent town on Kennedy Flats, a cleared patch in the wilderness. Less than four months after Leech had found gold, there were six stores, three hotels and thirty saloons, as he said, "in a locality never hitherto reached by white men and in all probability never by natives."

Close to $200,000 worth of gold was found in the area. Then, as quickly as it was born, Leechtown died. For his discovery, Governor Kennedy rewarded Leech $200. The elusiveness of a fortune in gold is emphasized by the fact that the claims of the men who ventured from Victoria averaged less than $100 per man over three years!

Aside from two mines near Ladysmith that produced gold, silver and copper ore in the 1890s, there was little mining excitement on Vancouver Island until 1935, when gold was discovered by some fishermen near the west coast port of Zeballos.

There is some suggestion that gold was discovered here before this — in 1791. A west coast priest, Father Terhaar, doing research in Madrid, found a receipt for $750,000 in gold shipped from the north west Pacific. The Spanish were driven from the area in 1795 by the English, who were anxious to control the fur trade. It is a fascinating thought that they may have sailed with a million dollars worth of gold, and the secret of Zeballos.

With the rush of 1936 the population reached 1,500. Gold values had jumped from $20 per ounce to $35 with the Depression, and six mines opened quickly. They did not last long; the most successful, the Privateer, closed in 1948. More than 166,000 tons of ore had been extracted. Zeballos was left to the loggers.

There are many Indian legends formerly interpreted as legends of gold: enormous deposits in the lost Indian village beyond Zeballos, buried under a fallen mountain in the valley of the Thunderbird; the river of gold and a "King's Tomb" in the crater of Mount Conuma in the Nootka district; the stream paved with gold near Forbidden Plateau. Students of Indian legends now interpret these references to wealth differently — as traditional secrets to spiritual wealth. An old miner is said to have returned from the Plateau with a pail full of nuggets, so perhaps the legends are more than figurative.

There was surprisingly little interest in developing a lumber industry on Vancouver Island prior to the early 1900s. On the early-settled southern end of the Island only two small water-powered sawmills had been constructed, one by John Muir of Sooke and the other on the Hudson's Bay

Company's Millstream Farm in Esquimalt. Yet the demand for lumber was high. San Francisco was in the midst of a building boom, and shipbuilding nations were seeking alternative sources to their diminishing supply of Riga spars from the Baltic area. In 1853, 18 ships carried piles for the wharves and lumber for the houses of San Francisco.

The gold rush brought a building boom in Victoria; as many as 30 buildings might be started in a single day. However, not all their timber was supplied from the Island. Victoria became a lucrative market for the Puget Sound loggers to the south.

Captain Edward Stamp was one of the first Victoria businessmen to invest heavily in forestry. "He built sawmills in outrageous places..." — Alberni was an outrageous place for a sawmill when Captain Stamp started production in 1861 after selling a cargo of magnificent Douglas spars in Britain. But the British Navy had rated the quality of the Island firs higher than those of the Baltic region, and soon Stamp had to build his own ships to meet the demand for lumber. He sold the mill the following year, 1862, to move to Burrard Inlet. Near the end of 1864 the Alberni Mill was closed because of a scarcity of convenient logs.

Then steam power was harnessed and the strange contraption called a steam or road donkey appeared. Its purpose was to pull logs over skids to where the donkey was sited. Up to a mile of cable would be pulled to the cuttings by horses and then hooked to the logs. The churning steam engine then wound the cable and logs in. The first donkey used in British Columbia appeared near Chemainus in 1900.

The next improvement was to lay light steel rails on the skids and tow the logs with a locomotive. Bell wheels on the engines made it practicable to use wooden poles for tracks in some locations. Riding those first tracks was a dangerous business: the brakeman rode the logs and applied hand brakes on the engineer's signal. Accidents were many, and eventually air brakes became mandatory. Geared locomotives were introduced to cope with the heavy grades. The three-cylinder Shay locomotives and two-cylinder Climaxes were the most popular of the logging locomotives.

These pre-war locomotives led long and productive lives; some survived late into the 1960s. The Bloedel Company's engine "One Spot" criss-crossed the Island from 1911 into the fifties before being shipped to the Philippines.

The locomotive speeded the timber harvest but efficiency dwindled as the branch lines expanded. Then came the truck. Today railways are confined to major routes while the large truck fleets haul the trees down the winding, steep logging roads of the Island.

As the forestry industry grew, huge amounts of capital were required, and the small family mills were consolidated into large corporations.

The growth of MacMillan Bloedel Limited exemplifies the vast change in the forest Industry. Their Menzies Bay camp, north of Campbell River, had a typical growth pattern. Logger campsites were built in 1925 and when the tree harvest was reaped the camps were moved. By 1940, trains were hauling timber from the shores of Brewster Lake. In 1951, trucks were brought in. By this time, logging was a basic aspect of a complex industry. Techological advances which followed World War II led to an incredible growth in the processing of raw timber, and capital investment was high. MacMillan Bloedel, which resulted from the merger of three large companies in the 1950s, pioneered much of that growth. The company now has logging and/or sawmill operations in Port Hardy, Kelsey Bay, Menzies Bay, Franklin River, Sproat Lake and Chemainus. Port Alberni is the central site of multi-million dollar mills to produce pulp and paper, kraft paper, shingles and other products.

Forest fires have long been the enemy of the industry. A fire which started near Campbell River in 1938 was probably the worst of the many that have ravaged the forests of the Island. After two dry months, fire broke out in early July and went on a 40-mile rampage. Batallions of loggers, navy men from Esquimalt, and resident volunteers fought the blaze, some going without food, sleep or water. By the end of July, 2,000 men were fighting the inferno that consumed up to seven miles per day. In 18 days, 200 square miles of forest were lost. More than 300 people fled their homes, and the loss of wildlife was immense. Despite increased safety measures, the problem remains — by 1950 there was an average of 1,700 forest fires per year in British Columbia, more than half caused by man — and forest fire fighting is the only service for which all able-bodied men are liable to conscription.

View of Nanaimo in 1862.
Provincial Archives, Victoria.

Loading coal at the infamous #1 shaft in Nanaimo in 1910.
Vancouver Public Library.

Smelter shift at Ladysmith's Tyee smelter, 1904.
Provincial Archives, Victoria.

Nanaimo; sacking coal for shipment to Alaska.
Provincial Archives, Victoria.

The first log cabin on the Leech River at the Mountain
Rose claim in the 1860s. The men who lived under its roof
were as rough as its construction.
Provincial Archives, Victoria.

The Reserve mine at Nanaimo.
Provincial Archives, Victoria.

Robert Dunsmuir made millions with two business
principles: to use other people's money and retain effective
control — particularly against the miners' union.

The limited coal supply on the west coast created such a
strong demand for Nanaimo reserves that before this
wharf was constructed in 1858, sailing ships were taking on
coal from canoes.
Vancouver Public Library.

A smiling show of military confidence at the Ladysmith
depot during the miner's strike, 1913.
Provincial Archives, Victoria.

Crowd at the pit head waiting for news of explosion
survivors. Only 7 of 157 left this Nanaimo coal mine alive
the afternoon of May 3, 1887.
Provincial Archives, Victoria.

Entrance to the Privateer mine at Zeballos, August 1939.
Provincial Archives, Victoria.

Mae West Avenue, Zeballos. Hollywood glamour in name if not in style
Provincial Archives, Victoria.

The Island's first-growth red cedars were so enormous that
they could not be made to fall cleanly from a cut at waist
height; the fallers had to elevate the reach of their axes.
Vancouver Public Library.

Captain Edward Stamp had both admirers and detractors of the role he played in the development of B.C. He rarely finished what he started but had a great gift as a promoter and gathered the needed British financing to start lumber mills on the Alberni Inlet and later at Hastings Mill (today's Vancouver).

In Nanaimo around 1875, an ox team pulls a wagonload of logs.
Vancouver Public Library.

The Chemainus River brought these log booms to their destination, a thriving mill.
Provincial Archives, Victoria.

The ten-ton Nanaimo, a mighty mite in the ranks of
locomotives, was the third engine to see service on
Vancouver Island. Engineer J. K. Hickman dangles a leg.
Provincial Archives, Victoria.

Dragged to the rails by steam donkeys, timber cargoes
were hauled by train to company log dumps like this one
at Chemainus.
Provincial Archives, Victoria.

This steam donkey (left) was one of the Island's first. It has
pulled logs from their felling point towards a locomotive,
the usual means of transporting logs at this time.
Provincial Archives, Victoria.

The crew of the Victoria Lumber and Manufacturing
Company at Cowichan Lake, near one of their raised —
but probably still damp — bunkhouses.
Vancouver Public Library.

A crew returns to this portable International Lumber
Company camp aboard an old passenger coach pulled by
a Shay steam locomotive.

Vancouver Public Library.

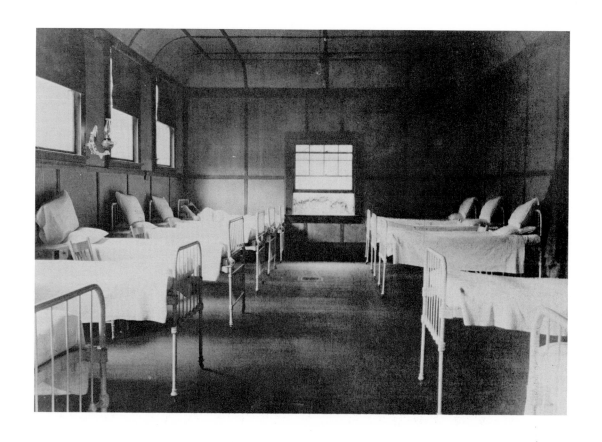

A casualty (or perhaps a model) rests in the Hastings
Sawmill Camp hospital at Rocky Bay, 1919.
Vancouver Public Library.

Constructed itself of timber, this Wood & English mill
processes a huge log at Englewood.
Vancouver Public Library.

With shining oil cloth on the tables and shiny apples
displayed on the inverted coffee cups, the dining hall of
the Wood & English logging camp near Englewood puts on
its best face for the photographer.
Vancouver Public Library.

The first paper plant on the Island was erected on the
Somass River near Port Alberni in 1894.
Provincial Archives, Victoria.

This Port Alberni mill of Bloedel, Stewart & Welch Ltd.
became the base of the pulp and paper operations of
MacMillan Bloedel Company during the 1950s.
Provincial Archives, Victoria.

The barque *Helene* made regular trips between these coal
bunkers in Nanaimo and the docks of San Francisco.
Provincial Archives, Victoria.

When Captain Cook left the shores of Friendly Cove in 1779 to sail to Macao with sea otter pelts in his cargo, he was unaware what riches he carried.

In 1784 Captain Hanna showed that fortunes were to be made by trading with the Indians when he sold 560 otter pelts in the Orient. Captain Strange, two years later, made a fat profit on 600 skins, and the year after that Barkley in the *Imperial Eagle* collected 800. Captains Dixon and Portland worked together to trade for more than 2,500 pelts. It was not long before the "Boston Men" arrived, led by Robert Gray in the *Columbia.* John Meares came from the Far East at this time.

By 1802 there were 42 English and American ships plying the coast, and they took 15,000 skins; the Russians took probably another 10,000.

The Indians had hunted the otter with harpoons, but the Europeans began using high-powered rifles. Sharpshooters in small boats would approach the herds and because the inquisitive animals would often swim towards the boats, shooting them was easy. In 1911, when otters were rarely sighted and bordered on extinction, Japan, Great Britain (representing Canada), Russia and the United States banned killing them.

For years they were rarely seen, but in 1938 a small herd appeared along the California coast. One herd on Copper Island in the North Pacific is well protected by the Soviet government, but it does not seem likely that sea otter herds will ever play on the shores of Vancouver Island again.

Seal hunting was another story of greedy slaughter, but when in 1874 Captain William Spring of Victoria sailed his schooner, *Favorite,* to the Bering Sea in search of seal, he opened one of the most colourful as well as barbarous eras on the west coast.

Not long afterward, the sealer's bowler was a common sight around the harbour; at one time the thriving Victoria sealing fleet numbered more than 100 schooners. Pelagic or open sea sealing was a dangerous life, and the men who chose it were a rugged breed. Ships raced each other to the far-off sealing grounds, and competing crews fought in harbour bars. On various voyages, men mutinied against brutal discipline; battled gales and violent seas; even defied the United States Navy.

The annual exodus to the Japanese sealing grounds was not only a commercial but also a sporting event. Many of the two-schooner races of 1895 were close, and that of the *Agnes Macdonald* and the *E. B. Marvin* was no exception. Captain Cutler did not take the *Agnes Macdonald's* jib boom from its lashings during the entire crossing, and won $250 in gold by a scant two hours. The *Casco* gave the *Diana* a day's start, but dropped anchor in Yokohama with a winning margin of five minutes. No other schooner could touch the refitted opium smuggler, *Vera* (formerly the *Halcyon*), which crossed the sea to Yokohama in 48 days.

On a previous visit to Japan, $50,000 worth of opium had been confiscated from the elegant 74-foot *Halcyon.*

Only the strongest of men could be a sealer captain. Such a man was Captain Jacobson. In the early years he induced Indians to join his ship, often, it is said, by force.

Like the otters, the seals became scarce, especially after rifles were used, for some three quarters of the shot seals sank before the hunters could reach them.

Soon Jacobson and three other persistent oldtimers captained the only Victoria sealing schooners. The 1911 agreement outlawed pelagic sealing, and the colourful fleet rotted in the Victoria harbour.

Although the international whaling industry peaked in 1846, when about 900, mainly American, ships sailed the seas, it was 1869 before a whaling station was started at Whaletown, British Columbia, by a James Douglas — not the governor. During the 1870s the industry went into a sharp decline after a large segment of the Pacific fleet of whalers was trapped in an early freeze in the Bering Sea. The availability of substitute oils also resulted in lessening demand for whale fat during the 1890s. However, the industry rallied briefly when during the first decade of this century permanent stations were established at Barkley Sound and Coal Harbour for the hunting of sperm and blue whales.

Factory ships, especially from other nations on the Pacific Rim, made their appearance in the twenties. Their greater yields led to depletion of Antarctic whale populations. British Columbia whalers found their local grounds becoming all too popular with the Japanese and Russians. In 1946 the International Whaling Convention agreed to conserve many species, setting minimum lengths for all species and protecting females with calves. Policing of the Convention was not all it should have been in the 1940s, although it is now better managed.

Commercial fishing dates back to the earliest days of Indian bartering with the Hudson's Bay Company. Among the pioneers of the Island area were Captain William Spring and Captain Hugh McKay. Their Becher Bay Fisheries salted 400 barrels of salmon per year in the late 1850s for shipment to the Sandwich Islands. A second plant, west of Sooke, soon followed. But it was this century before fishing became an important resource industry in the province.

In 1904, when fish traps were made legal, two were placed off Sooke, where the salmon made their annual run towards the Fraser. The nets stretched 15 miles on either side of Sooke Harbour; their presence was a contentious issue for years. Fish traps are now banned everywhere in British Columbia but at Sooke.

Today highly automated Soviet and Japanese fleets of seiners fish off the British Columbia coast. Ecologists warn that many species are endangered, pointing to the meagre catches of British Columbia fleets. The conflicting demands of man and nature remain.

During the 19th century the Royal Navy protected British commercial and territorial interests in the Pacific Northwest. Its presence allowed the Hudson's Bay Company to dominate the fur trade and to control immigration during the 1858 gold stampede. Esquimalt was deemed a harbour of strategic importance to the Admiralty, and after war with Russia broke out in 1854, Vancouver Island became a home for the Pacific Fleet.

Thus the corvette, HMS *Satellite*, enforced the immigration regulations of Governor Douglas at the mouth of the Fraser and provided a British show of force on San Juan Island during the 1859 "Pig War." (Territorial claims to San Juan Island were being made by both the United States and Britain during the 1850s. Tensions reached their peak when an American sympathizer killed a neighbouring farmer's pig. The aggrieved farmer sought redress from the Victoria courts. Ensuing actions led both the British and the Americans to occupy the island by force to show their respective flags. Far-off diplomats settled the issue in 1872.)

In 1862 the Pacific headquarters of the Navy was moved from Valparaiso, Chile, to Esquimalt, but it was 1887 before the long-overdue Esquimalt drydock was completed, by then with Canadian government funds. In its first seven years of operation it serviced 70 British warships and 24 merchant ships. The batteries of Signal and Fort Rodd Hill were constructed in 1895.

By 1901 there were only eight Royal Navy ships in the Pacific, and in 1905 the Pacific Fleet was abolished. Canada became the reluctant defender of her own west coast.

The treacherous coast from Port Renfrew to Barkley Sound is called "the graveyard of the Pacific." Between the losses of the *William* in 1854, and the 8,500-ton *Vanlene*, a freighter carrying Japanese cars to Vancouver in the spring of 1972, no fewer than 58 vessels have been wrecked on this rocky coast.

One of the earliest mishaps occurred in 1859, when the small American brig, *Swiss Boy*, sought refuge in Barkley Sound. Captain Welden and his crew of eight were over-powered by an excited band of Haida pirates who robbed them and damaged the ship. After the American crew returned to Victoria, Captain Prevost and HMS *Satellite* investigated. He found that the Indians had acted against a "foreign invader" in the name and honour of King George; that damage to the vessel and cargo was less than $500 and that the *Swiss Boy* was a waterlogged old hulk which should never have been allowed to sea. His decision was partly political, and only partly based on fact. Americans, above all, were considered to be foreign invaders.

Lighthouses on the west coast of the Island and along the coast of the Olympic Peninsula to the south prevented many shipwrecks — and caused a few. In the early 1900s new navigational codes were being introduced and poor communication meant outdated charts. New lights were often uncharted, and their unexpected presence often caused confusion in the wheelhouse, with resultant disasters.

On January 22, 1906, the *Valencia*, a 1,598-ton passenger steamer heading for Victoria from San Francisco, misjudged its position by 40 miles and steered directly into the sharp reef south of Pachena Point. Only 38 of the 165 aboard survived. A commission attributed the wreck to bad weather, navigational incompetence, improper rescue efforts, inaccessible and inadequate life saving facilities ashore, and the lack of a lighthouse on Pachena Point. The Pachena light was constructed, and exactly three years later, the 698-ton four-masted schooner *Soquel* was driven off course while approaching Cape Flattery, the southern shore of the Strait of Juan de Fuca. Captain Henningsen, steering for the Strait of San Juan, aimed a middle course between the two visible lights, Cape Beale to the north (which he took as Carmanah light) and what he thought was Cape Flattery to the south. It was the new Pachena light to his south, however, and the *Soquel* at full speed hit Seabird Rocks at high tide. After the heroic efforts of the Bamfield lifeboat crew transferred survivors to the shelter of a nearby ship, it was found that the captain's wife and child had been swept overboard to their death. It was the captain's last voyage.

In another near-disastrous incident, the 853-ton barque *Coloma* found herself helplessly drifting off the jagged shore of isolated Cape Beale in early December, 1906. Though the light-keepers, Tom and Minnie Paterson, spotted her, their telephone line to Bamfield was down. Tom could not leave the light, but Minnie did; in a howling storm she waded through the waist-deep lagoon to the mainland, then scrambled over five miles of fallen trees, slimy rocks, mud and soggy beaches in search of aid.

She reach the house of the telephone lineman, but his wife was there alone. The two women launched a small boat and rowed to the lighthouse supply craft, *Quadra*, with their story. Little was left of the *Coloma* when the *Quadra* arrived. The bow was slashed open, the cargo of lumber scattered, and the crew clustered helplessly in the shelter of the deckhouse. All were saved, and Minnie became known as Heroine of the Cape Beale Light.

Until 1958 no single channel off the Island was more feared than the Seymour Straits, where a submerged fang known as Ripple Rock disembowelled many a ship. It required history's largest non-nuclear explosion to blast 40 feet from the hazard.

One of the legendary Nootka warriors, aboard a sealing
ship in Victoria harbour.
Provincial Archives, Victoria.

The usually lively, appealing sea otter was drawn around 1778 in this petrified pose, eloquent of the fact that Europeans valued it much more dead than alive.
Provincial Archives, Victoria.

The sealing fleet in Victoria harbour at the turn of the century.
Vancouver Public Library.

Sea lions were not prized for their pelts as were seals, but this specimen, perhaps old or sick, was taken during the hunt. The seal pup seems to be thriving.
Provincial Archives, Victoria.

Captain Larsen of the *SS St Lawrence* shows in this 1908 photograph how mechanical Goliaths replaced canoe-borne Davids when white men took over whaling on the Pacific coast.
Provincial Archives, Victoria.

By 1910, the whale oil shipped from Victoria in these barrels was being used for luxury products — symbolized unwittingly in this scene by the seated officer's lap dog.
Vancouver Public Library.

The whaler's catch: an 80-foot blue whale, here being flensed.
Vancouver Public Library.

This salmon weir on the Cowichan River trapped much of
the food supply for the nearby village until lumber booms
from up-river forced it out.
Provincial Archives, Victoria.

As the fish nets of the Sooke traps are pulled in, a harvest
of salmon comes to the surface.
Provincial Archives, Victoria.

The *Coloma* in distress off Cape Beale in December 1906.
The storm which drove her onto the rocks made rescue —
and photography — difficult.
Provincial Archives, Victoria.

Captain John Thomas Walbran, for 13 years captain of the
lighthouse tender and supply ship *Quadra,* had brought the
ship himself from Britain around Cape Horn.

In storms that had overcome ships many times larger,
these boats went to the rescue through high surf off Tofino.
Provincial Archives, Victoria.

Even the old SS *Quadra*, which had had many roles in
government service, found a new career during Prohibition
As a Rum Row mother ship, the grand old lady stored
many gallons of contraband in her iron hull.
Provincial Archives, Victoria.

The *Beryl G* was no more infamous than any other rum
runner until the night that hijackers killed her captain,
Bill Miller, and his son, off Sidney Island.
Provincial Archives, Victoria.

In the days of the *Valencia*, steamers took aboard as many passengers as possible. A crowd like this embarked from San Francisco in January 1906; 117 were lost with her off the west coast of the Island.
Provincial Archives, Victoria.

Since 1908, ships entering Victoria's Inner Harbour have been greeted by two stone sentinels, "The Empress" and "Parliament."
Provincial Archives, Victoria.

The SS *Motor Princess* was a new kind of vessel. In 1923 the first passengers drove their treasured automobiles aboard the diesel-powered ferry, and Captain James Troup's fleet was on its way.
Provincial Archives, Victoria.

The Canadian Pacific Navigation Company's *Princess Victoria* steams across the Strait of Georgia in postcard splendour. Captain James Troup launched the Princess fleet to bring Seattle and Vancouver clientele to the then-new Empress Hotel.

Provincial Archives, Victoria.

The squarish upturned prow of this cedar canoe marks it
as a modest everyday relative of the awesome whaling and
war canoes of earlier years. Cargo canoes served local
transport all around the Island well into the 1860s.
Vancouver Public Library.

The first Esquimalt & Nanaimo Railway train to enter the
new downtown terminal in 1888 represented fulfillment of
the first federal promise valued by Victorians. The arrival
of the CPR in Vancouver a year earlier failed to enhance
national feeling on the Island.
Provincial Archives, Victoria.

In 1860 it took from four to six months to sail the 17,000-mile journey from England to Vancouver Island via Cape Horn. The fare ranged from 30 to 70 pounds, children travelling at half price; goods were shipped for six pounds per ton. The faster route was by ship to Panama, by train across the 42-mile isthmus, and by American steamer to San Francisco and Vancouver Island. This route, although slightly more expensive, took 14 to 20 days to Panama, five hours to the Pacific, another two weeks to San Francisco and five days more to Vancouver Island.

In 1862 the only alternative routes from the Atlantic were four overland routes to San Francisco and then up the coast. Except for the Overlanders who established new trails across the Prairies and through the Rockies, the ship remained the major means of transport.

The *Empress of India* in 1891 opened an era in world trade for British Columbia. She was the first of the three "White Empresses" built by the CPR to open Pacific trade and bring business to the new transcontinental railway. Each of the 6,000-ton ships, 485 feet in length, carried 450 passengers and with twin propellers could manage 17½ knots. On its maiden voyage, the *Empress of India* sailed from Yokohama to Vancouver Island in 12 days only to find insufficient docking facilities. This problem was soon rectified and for 25 years the three ships, named after the monarchs of Japan, India and China, sailed the Pacific, bringing mail and opium from Hong Kong, silk from Japan, and passengers from around the world. Silk cargoes valued as high as $10 million passed through Victoria and Vancouver enroute to New York.

Larger sister ships, the *Empress of Russia* and *Empress of Asia*, appeared in 1914, but were soon enlisted for war service.

After World War I, political strategy and high unemployment spurred a new drydock construction program. The 1,150-foot drydock at Esquimalt, with its 1,200-ton gates, was the largest in the world. In 1942 it was the only one in the Pacific able to accommodate the *Queen Elizabeth* for refitting as a troop carrier.

During the 1940s the age of sail ended in Victoria. Passing reminders were the *Melanope* and *Pamir*. The former spent 30 years as a clipper ship, but in 1906 joined the growing number of sailing ships being converted to barges.

The *Melanope* carried coal from Ladysmith to Vancouver harbour for the furnaces of the Empress fleet until 1946, when she was sunk as part of the Royston breakwater. That same year, the 3,000-ton *Pamir*, a German nitrate clipper in the early 1900s, sailed into the harbour. She was the last of the old sailing ships to visit Victoria.

In 1902 the first trans-Pacific telegraph cable was laid from Australia to Bamfield on the west coast of Vancouver Island. A second cable spanned the 7,800 miles in 1926.

In 1861, after competition had reduced rates to one third of the 1858 level, the fare for the 82-mile trip from Victoria to the mainland was $5 and freight was $3 per ton. Gold seekers going from the Island to Hope or Yale paid $10 for passage and $20 per ton for baggage. Several steamers ran across the Georgia Strait in summer months, but there were only three trips per week during the winter.

After coal operations began, the steamer *Maude* connected Nanaimo to Burrard Inlet, conveying the mail, freight and passengers in 4½ hours.

The paddlewheelers which connected Vancouver Island and the mainland were flat-bottomed craft, about 125 by 30 feet, similar to those made famous on the Mississippi River. In fact, these sternwheelers were used more in British Columbia than in any other part of North America.

Competitive steamer service continued from Victoria to New Westminster and up the Fraser until 1886, when the Canadian Pacific Navigation Company was formed and introduced the SS *Islander* to the Vancouver-Victoria run. The paddlewheelers were the main means of getting to the mainland during the flurry of the Klondike rush and into the 20th century.

In 1903 a new ferry called the *Victoria* introduced an efficient service between Sidney and the mouth of the Fraser. Then with the completion of the Empress Hotel in 1906, Captain James Troup introduced a luxury ferry service to connect Seattle, Vancouver and Victoria. This service has continued until today, interrupted only when the CPR ships were designated for troop service in the two world wars.

In 1923 Captain Troup put the 170-foot, diesel-powered *Motor Princess* into service. The first of the auto ferries, it was able to carry 40 cars and 250 people.

The CPR service continued until 1959, when the fleet of auto ferries was strike bound. Premier W.A.C. Bennett acted quickly and took over this vital service, added ships, and expanded docking facilities to build the world's largest ferry fleet, with more than a score of ships.

The year 1919 saw the first plane flight from Vancouver to Victoria. The high cost of terminal facilities deterred development of landing strips on the Island, and the Victoria airport remained a secondary terminus for Vancouver's international air traffic, with 11 daily flights to the Island by 1949.

The first regular air service between Vancouver and Victoria started in 1932, and since then Air Canada and smaller regional services have continued to provide regular and charter service across the Georgia Strait.

Many Island communities which had been settled by ship remained accessible only by water transport, although informal communications systems functioned well from 1845 onwards — so much so that political news was known along the whole east coast within 24 hours in the late 1850s.

Indian dugouts served well as local passenger transports — they first carried "King George men" to the Nanaimo coal fields, and took the Leech party up to the Sooke river to gold discoveries. Later, steamers like the *Beaver* and later *HMS Quadra* played an important role in supplying staples to isolated coastal communities. Regular passage to Nanaimo from Victoria could be had by 1860 on a small screw steamer, *Cariboo Fly*; the fare was $5.

In 1865 mail went the 70-mile trip twice a week on the *Emily Harris*. Less frequent trips to Barkley Sound were available. Roads were developed only in the southeast corner of Vancouver Island by then. Wagon roads to Esquimalt and Sooke and over 35 miles to Cowichan had been built from Victoria.

By the late 1880s there was a stagecoach running from Victoria to Nanaimo with roadhouses along the route. It was soon extended to Parksville and Alberni, the Nanaimo-Alberni trip taking three days. The Esquimalt and Nanaimo Railway opened in August, 1886, the last spike driven in by Prime Minister John A. Macdonald at Shawnigan Lake. The train ran at 30 miles per hour and made 11 stops along the route. Before the line was sold to Canadian Pacific Railways in 1905 it was extended to Alberni and Courtenay.

One type of vehicle which fell victim to inadequate roads was the traction engine or road steamer. Francis Barnard brought four Thomson Patent Road Steamers and six engineers to Victoria in 1871. They failed tests to haul freight to the Cariboo, as the soft rubber of their wheels could not stand up to the rocky roads.

They went the same way as Frank Laumeister's 23 Bactrian camels a decade earlier. Most went on to the Cariboo after frightening every horse they met along the road from Esquimalt to Victoria. A few, however, remained near Victoria to do farm work.

By 1910 the horseless carriage was a common sight, and adventuresome motorists were attempting the four-hour trip from Victoria to Nanaimo. Joe Sayward, a prosperous Victoria lumberman, received the first city traffic summons and a $25 fine for exceeding ten miles per hour on a bridge. In 1912 there were only 175 auto automoblies in British Columbia. Fifteen years later, there were nearly 30,000 when the province converted from left to right lane driving. Incredibly, there were no auto accidents on Vancouver Island that night.

Victoria's first flying machine was built in 1911 by William G. Gibson, although there is no evidence that it got off the ground. The urgency of gold seekers to get to the Zeballos rush in 1939 led to the first Island air routes. The alternative was a six-day cruise of the CPR's *Princess Maquenna*, and impatient miners made steady use of Ginger Coote's daily air service.

Even today most of the Island's west coast is accessible only by chartered plane or coastal steamer or over logging roads, although two recent highways now reach the Tofino area and Gold River. Highways extend beyond Campbell River to Kelsey Bay on the east coast, but it is still impossible to drive the length of the Island on public highways. The B.C. Ferry is the only public link to the northern end of the Island.

The sea retains a strong influence over daily life. It both challenges and serves the Island residents. The portrait of future periods will no doubt show that, as in the past, the sea has made the difference in the way things are done in this distinctive part of North America.

"Old" Martin's ornate silver-framed hearse stops at the
corner of Broughton and Langley streets as it might have
done in one of many processions in the 1890s.
Provincial Archives, Victoria.

A fashionable excursion departs from Bray's Livery Stable
in the mild Victoria weather enjoyed best from open
horse-drawn carriages.
Provincial Archives, Victoria.

The Island's first motoring families did not have to drive
far out of town to find forest like this.
Vancouver Public Library.

"At Beacon Hill," Emily Carr's commentary — pictorial and verbal — on the motor car:
"We are not yet quite reconciled to the automobiles. They alarm the horses; the horses alarm the ladies; the ladies alarm the babies; the babies alarm the dogs; and much general confusion ensues."
Provincial Archives, Victoria.

In 1910, an automobile was novel enough to enter a parade undecorated, but these passengers preferred to exhibit theirs with blankets, trinkets and smiles.
Vancouver Public Library.

The Indians called Emily Carr, painter and writer, Klee Wyck, laughing one. She undertook hazardous travels to their villages and left in her paintings a legacy of Indian life. In this photo she is standing in her caravan which, in the summers 1933 to 37, she moved into the forests to paint in solitude.

Provincial Archives, Victoria.

As foreign to the modern eye as Laumeister's camels to the
Island — a steam-powered truck.
Provincial Archives, Victoria.

The microbus of yesterday: Sisco's Fast Express service in
Ladysmith.
Provincial Archives, Victoria.

NOTICE TO AUTOMOBILISTS.

Rules of the Road in British Columbia.

In order to avoid confusion and possible accidents, the attention of all Motorists is directed to the "Rules of the Road" in this Province:—

1. On meeting a vehicle keep to the left.
2. On overtaking and passing a vehicle pass to the right.
3. Drive always on left hand side of the road.

BRITISH COLUMBIA AUTOMOBILE LAWS.

Visiting motorists are requested to comply with the provisions of the "Motor Vehicles Act," which provides that all automobiles must be registered and a permit obtained from the Superintendent of Provincial Police at Victoria.

DANGER.

Owing to the narrow and winding nature of some roads, which at many places abound in sudden, sharp turns (around which it is impossible to see, owing to dense vegetation, high banks, etc.), it is necessary at times to drive with great caution.

SPEED.

Within Incorporated Cities and Towns, NOT MORE THAN TEN MILES AN HOUR. Outside of any City or Town, NOT MORE THAN FIFTEEN MILES AN HOUR.

F. S. HUSSEY,
Superintendent Provincial Police.

Provincial Police Department,
Victoria, B. C.

The rules of the road before 1927, when right-lane travel began.
Provincial Archives, Victoria.

Like the Garry oaks behind this gathering of proud owners, horseless carriages were confined at first to the southeastern Island. Elsewhere, road development was slow to come.
Provincial Archives, Victoria.

MV *Chinook* was the sleek flag ship of the pioneering Black Ball Transport company. B.C. Ferries rechristened her *Sechelt Queen*.
Provincial Archives, Victoria.

The successful launching of this pusher biplane in
Vancouver, 1910, preceded Victoria's first flying machine
by a year.
Provincial Archives, Victoria.

Victoria's Oak Bay trolley line offered the summer treat of
this open air car, often called the Golfer's Special. The
line's traffic superintendant, Henry Gibson, take a fond
proprietary stance at the extreme right.
Provincial Archives, Victoria.

VICTO
1

EXPLANATORY.

1. Russell's Station.
2. Marine Hospital.
3. Provincial Jail.
4. Victoria Rice Mill.
5. Albion Iron Works.
6. Ocean Dock.
7. Freight Depot E. & N. R. R.
8. Hudson Bay Co's Store.

9. Canadian Pacific Nav. Co's Office.
10. Rice Mill's Wharf.
11. Spratt's Wharf.
12. Porter Bro's Wharf.
13. Janion's Wharf.
14. R. P. Pritchet & Co's Wharf.
15. Turner Beeton & Co.
       (O. R. & N. Co.)

16. C. P. N. Co's Wharf.
17. Masonic Temple.
18. St. John's Church.
19. Wesley Church.
20. Baptist Church.
21. George Road Methodist Church.
22. City Hall.
23. Law Courts.

24. First Presbyterian Church.
25. Temperance Hall.
26. Deluge Fire Hall.
27. Colonists Office.
28. Custom House.
29. St. James' Church.
30. Bank British Columbia.
31. Odd Fellow's Hall.